LGBTQ SENSITIVITY

Table Of Contents

INTRODUCTION

In the rapidly evolving landscape of healthcare, it is imperative for providers to offer compassionate, informed, and sensitive care to all patients. Among the diverse patient populations that healthcare providers encounter, LGBTQ individuals often face unique challenges and disparities that can significantly impact their health outcomes. As a healthcare provider, understanding these challenges and knowing how to address them can make a profound difference in the lives of your patients.

"Compassionate Care: A Comprehensive Guide to LGBTQ Sensitivity for Healthcare Providers" is designed to equip healthcare professionals with the knowledge and tools they need to deliver culturally competent care to LGBTQ patients. This book is not just about acquiring factual knowledge; it's about fostering empathy, building trust, and creating an inclusive environment where all patients feel safe and respected.

The journey begins with a foundational understanding of LGBTQ identities and terminologies. Many healthcare providers may find themselves unfamiliar with the vast spectrum of gender identities and sexual orientations, and this lack of understanding can inadvertently lead to miscommunication or even discrimination..

The historical context and evolution of LGBTQ rights provide a backdrop for understanding the systemic challenges and prejudices that this community has faced. This knowledge is crucial for recognizing the ongoing struggles and the importance of advocating for LGBTQ rights within the healthcare system. By embracing the principles and practices outlined in these pages, you can make a significant impact on the health and well-being of your LGBTQ patients. Together, we can create a healthcare system that truly serves everyone with dignity, respect, and compassion.

MODULE ONE

LESSON ONE: UNDERSTANDING LGBTQ IDENTITIES AND TERMINOLOGIES

The foundation of providing sensitive and informed care to LGBTQ patients starts with understanding the diverse identities and terminologies associated with this community. The LGBTQ acronym stands for Lesbian, Gay, Bisexual, Transgender, and Queer/Questioning, but the spectrum of identities it represents is much broader.

Defining Sexual Orientation and Gender Identity

Sexual orientation refers to an individual's physical, romantic, and/or emotional attraction to people of the same gender, different gender, or multiple genders. Common sexual orientations include heterosexual (attracted to the opposite gender), homosexual (attracted to the same gender), bisexual (attracted to two or more genders), and pansexual (attracted to all genders regardless of their sex or gender identity).

Gender identity, on the other hand, refers to an individual's deeply-felt sense of being male, female, a blend of both, or neither. It is important to distinguish gender identity from biological sex, which is based on physical characteristics such as chromosomes, hormone levels, and reproductive organs. Common gender identities include cisgender (gender identity matches the sex assigned at birth), transgender (gender identity differs from the sex assigned at birth), non-binary (gender identity doesn't fit within the traditional binary of male and female), and genderqueer (a term often used interchangeably with non-binary).

Pronouns and Their Importance

Pronouns are a key component of respectful communication. Using the correct pronouns for someone affirms their gender identity and shows respect. Common pronouns include "he/him," "she/her," and "they/them," but some individuals may use other pronouns such as "ze/hir." It is always best to ask someone their preferred pronouns and use them consistently.

Expanding the LGBTQ Acronym

The LGBTQ acronym is often expanded to include additional identities, reflecting the diverse and evolving nature of the community. These can include:

- LGBTQIA+: Adding Intersex (individuals born with physical sex characteristics that don't fit typical definitions of male or female) and Asexual (individuals who do not experience sexual attraction).
- 2S: Two-Spirit, a term used by some Indigenous cultures in North America to describe a person who embodies both masculine and feminine qualities.

Understanding Intersectionality

Intersectionality is a framework for understanding how various aspects of a person's identity (such as race, gender, sexual orientation, class, etc.) intersect and impact their experiences. For LGBTQ individuals, intersectionality can play a significant role in shaping their health outcomes and access to care. For example, a Black transgender woman may face different challenges and barriers compared to a white cisgender gay man. Recognizing these intersecting identities is crucial for providing comprehensive and sensitive care.

Myths and Misconceptions

There are many myths and misconceptions about LGBTQ identities that can contribute to stigma and discrimination. Some common misconceptions include:

- Believing that sexual orientation or gender identity is a choice.
- Assuming that all LGBTQ individuals have the same experiences or health needs.
- Thinking that being LGBTQ is a mental illness.

Dispelling these myths through education and awareness is an essential step in reducing stigma and providing better care.

The Importance of Cultural Competence

Cultural competence involves understanding and respecting the cultural differences and similarities within and between groups. For healthcare providers, cultural competence includes being aware of your own biases and prejudices, actively seeking to understand the experiences of LGBTQ patients, and adapting your care to meet their unique needs. This ongoing process requires a commitment to education, self-reflection, and empathy.

Understanding LGBTQ identities and terminologies is the first step towards providing compassionate and effective care. By familiarizing yourself with the diverse identities within the LGBTQ community, using respectful language, and recognizing the importance of intersectionality, you can create a more inclusive and supportive environment for all patients.

MODULE TWO

LESSON ONE: HISTORICAL CONTEXT AND THE EVOLUTION OF LGBTQ RIGHTS

The history of LGBTQ rights is a complex and multifaceted journey marked by periods of progress, setbacks, and ongoing struggles. Understanding this history is crucial for healthcare providers, as it provides context for the current challenges and disparities faced by LGBTQ individuals.

Early History and Pre-20th Century Attitudes

LGBTQ identities have existed throughout history, but attitudes towards them have varied greatly across different cultures and time periods. In many ancient societies, same-sex relationships and non-binary gender identities were often accepted or even revered. However, with the rise of certain religious and cultural norms, LGBTQ identities began to be stigmatized and criminalized.

The 20th Century: From Oppression to Activism

The 20th century saw significant changes in attitudes towards LGBTQ individuals, particularly in Western societies. The early part of the century was marked by widespread discrimination, criminalization, and pathologization of LGBTQ identities. However, the mid-20th century saw the rise of the LGBTQ rights movement, with landmark events such as the Stonewall Riots in 1969 sparking widespread activism and advocacy.

The HIV/AIDS Crisis and Its Impact

The HIV/AIDS crisis of the 1980s and 1990s had a profound impact on the LGBTQ community. The epidemic not only highlighted the health disparities faced by gay men but also galvanized the community to fight for better healthcare, research, and social support. The crisis also brought attention to the intersection of health and social justice, as LGBTQ activists worked to combat stigma and discrimination associated with the disease.

Legal and Policy Milestones

The late 20th and early 21st centuries saw significant legal and policy advances for LGBTQ rights. Key milestones include the decriminalization of homosexuality in many countries, the removal of homosexuality from the list of mental disorders by the American Psychiatric Association, and the legalization of same-sex marriage in numerous jurisdictions. These changes have had a profound impact on the lives of LGBTQ individuals and their access to healthcare.

Ongoing Challenges and the Road Ahead

Despite significant progress, many challenges remain for the LGBTQ community. Discrimination, stigma, and violence continue to affect the lives of LGBTQ individuals, particularly those who are also members of other marginalized groups. Healthcare providers must be aware of these ongoing issues and advocate for policies and practices that promote equality and inclusion.

The Role of Healthcare Providers in Advocacy

Healthcare providers have a unique role to play in advocating for LGBTQ rights and improving health outcomes. This can include advocating for inclusive policies within healthcare institutions, supporting LGBTQ health research, and working to reduce stigma and discrimination within the healthcare system. Providers can also engage in community outreach and education to promote awareness and acceptance of LGBTQ individuals.

The historical context of LGBTQ rights provides a vital backdrop for understanding the challenges and disparities faced by LGBTQ individuals today. By recognizing the progress that has been made and the work that still needs to be done, healthcare providers can better serve their LGBTQ patients and contribute to a more equitable and inclusive healthcare system.

MODULE THREE

LESSON ONE: HEALTH DISPARITIES AND CHALLENGES FACED BY LGBTQ INDIVIDUALS

LGBTQ individuals face a range of health disparities and challenges that can significantly impact their overall well-being. These disparities are often the result of a combination of social, economic, and environmental factors, as well as discrimination and stigma.

Mental Health Disparities

Mental health issues are prevalent in the LGBTQ community, with higher rates of depression, anxiety, and suicidal ideation compared to the general population. Factors contributing to these disparities include social stigma, discrimination, rejection by family and peers, and the stress associated with concealing one's identity.

Substance Use and Abuse

Substance use and abuse are also more common among LGBTQ individuals, particularly among those who face high levels of stress and discrimination. This includes higher rates of alcohol, tobacco, and drug use. Healthcare providers must be aware of these patterns and offer appropriate screening and interventions.

Sexual and Reproductive Health

LGBTQ individuals face unique challenges related to sexual and reproductive health. For example, lesbian and bisexual women may be less likely to receive regular gynecological care, and transgender individuals may face barriers to accessing gender-affirming care. Additionally, gay and bisexual men are at higher risk for HIV and other sexually transmitted infections (STIs).

Chronic Diseases and Physical Health

LGBTQ individuals may also experience higher rates of certain chronic diseases and physical health issues. For instance, research has shown that LGBTQ individuals are more likely to suffer from cardiovascular diseases, obesity, and certain cancers. These disparities can be attributed to a combination of behavioral, social, and healthcare-related factors.

Barriers to Healthcare Access

Barriers to healthcare access are a significant issue for many LGBTQ individuals. These can include financial barriers, lack of culturally competent providers, fear of discrimination, and lack of inclusive policies and practices within healthcare institutions. Addressing these barriers is essential for improving health outcomes in the LGBTQ community.

Intersectionality and Health Disparities

The concept of intersectionality is crucial for understanding the health disparities faced by LGBTQ individuals. For example, LGBTQ people of color may experience compounded discrimination and stigma that can further impact their health outcomes. Similarly, LGBTQ individuals with disabilities may face additional barriers to accessing care.

Strategies for Addressing Health Disparities

Addressing health disparities in the LGBTQ community requires a multifaceted approach. This can include:

- Providing culturally competent care: Ensuring that healthcare providers are trained to understand and respect LGBTQ identities and experiences.

- Promoting inclusive policies: Advocating for policies that support LGBTQ individuals, such as anti-discrimination protections and inclusive healthcare practices.
- Supporting mental health services: Expanding access to mental health services for LGBTQ individuals and addressing the unique stressors they face.
- Improving data collection: Collecting data on sexual orientation and gender identity to better understand and address health disparities.
- Engaging in community outreach: Working with LGBTQ organizations and communities to promote health and well-being.

The health disparities and challenges faced by LGBTQ individuals are significant and multifaceted. By understanding these disparities and implementing strategies to address them, healthcare providers can play a crucial role in improving the health and well-being of LGBTQ patients.

MODULE FIVE

LESSON ONE: CREATING A SAFE AND INCLUSIVE ENVIRONMENT IN HEALTHCARE SETTINGS

Creating a safe and inclusive environment is essential for ensuring that LGBTQ patients feel comfortable and respected when seeking care. This lesson provides practical strategies for healthcare providers to create such an environment.

Inclusive Language and Communication

Using inclusive language is a fundamental aspect of creating a welcoming environment. This includes:

- Using correct pronouns: Always ask for and use a patient's preferred pronouns.
- Avoiding assumptions: Do not make assumptions about a person's sexual orientation or gender identity based on their appearance or behavior.
- Using gender-neutral language: Use terms like "partner" instead of "husband" or "wife" unless you know the patient's preferred terminology.

Staff Training and Education

Providing training and education for all staff members is crucial for creating an inclusive environment. This can include:

- Cultural competence training: Offering training sessions on LGBTQ identities, health disparities, and inclusive practices.

- Regular updates: Ensuring that staff receive regular updates on new research, policies, and best practices related to LGBTQ healthcare.

Inclusive Policies and Procedures

Implementing inclusive policies and procedures can help ensure that all patients are treated with respect and dignity. This can include:

- Non-discrimination policies: Establishing and enforcing policies that prohibit discrimination based on sexual orientation, gender identity, and gender expression.
- Inclusive intake forms: Designing intake forms that allow patients to self-identify their sexual orientation and gender identity.
- Privacy and confidentiality: Ensuring that patient information is kept confidential and that staff understand the importance of privacy for LGBTQ patients.

Physical Environment and Facilities

The physical environment of a healthcare facility can also impact the comfort and safety of LGBTQ patients. Considerations include:

- Gender-neutral bathrooms: Providing gender-neutral or single-stall restrooms for patients and staff.
- Inclusive signage: Using signage that indicates an inclusive and welcoming environment, such as rainbow flags or "safe space" symbols.
- Accessible facilities: Ensuring that facilities are accessible to all patients, including those with disabilities.

Building Trust and Rapport

Building trust and rapport with LGBTQ patients is essential for providing effective care. Strategies include:

- Active listening: Listening to patients without judgment and validating their experiences.
- Empathy and compassion: Demonstrating empathy and compassion in all interactions with patients.
- Patient-centered care: Focusing on the individual needs and preferences of each patient and involving them in decision-making about their care.

Community Engagement and Outreach

Engaging with the LGBTQ community can help build trust and improve health outcomes. This can include:

- Partnering with LGBTQ organizations: Collaborating with local LGBTQ organizations to provide resources and support for patients.
- Participating in community events: Participating in LGBTQ events and initiatives to show support and build connections with the community.
- Providing educational resources: Offering educational resources and information on LGBTQ health topics to patients and the community.

Creating a safe and inclusive environment in healthcare settings is essential for ensuring that LGBTQ patients feel comfortable and respected. By implementing inclusive language, policies, and practices, providing staff training and education, and engaging with the community, healthcare providers can create a welcoming and supportive environment for all patients.

MODULE FIVE

LESSON ONE: LEGAL AND ETHICAL CONSIDERATIONS IN LGBTQ HEALTHCARE

Providing healthcare to LGBTQ patients involves navigating a complex landscape of legal and ethical considerations. Understanding these issues is essential for ensuring that your practice is not only compassionate but also compliant with legal standards.

Understanding Anti-Discrimination Laws

Anti-discrimination laws play a critical role in protecting LGBTQ individuals from discrimination in healthcare settings. These laws vary by country and region, but key provisions often include:

- Equal access: Ensuring that LGBTQ individuals have equal access to healthcare services without discrimination based on sexual orientation, gender identity, or gender expression.
- Non-discrimination policies: Implementing and enforcing policies that explicitly prohibit discrimination against LGBTQ patients and staff.

Informed Consent and Confidentiality

Informed consent and confidentiality are fundamental ethical principles in healthcare. For LGBTQ patients, these principles are particularly important:

- Informed consent: Ensuring that patients fully understand their treatment options and are involved in decision-making processes. This includes providing clear and comprehensive information about procedures, especially those related to gender-affirming care.

- Confidentiality: Protecting patient privacy is crucial. This includes safeguarding information about a patient's sexual orientation, gender identity, and any treatments related to their LGBTQ status. Breaches of confidentiality can lead to significant harm and loss of trust.

Legal Recognition of Gender Identity

Legal recognition of gender identity is a significant issue for transgender and non-binary individuals. Healthcare providers must be aware of the following:

- Legal documentation: Understanding the process for changing legal documents (such as birth certificates, driver's licenses, and medical records) to reflect a patient's gender identity.
- Insurance coverage: Navigating insurance policies to ensure coverage for gender-affirming treatments and procedures, which can vary widely depending on the jurisdiction and the specific insurance plan.

Ethical Considerations in Treatment

Ethical considerations in the treatment of LGBTQ patients include:

- Respect for autonomy: Respecting the autonomy of LGBTQ patients in making decisions about their own healthcare, including decisions about gender-affirming treatments.
- Non-maleficence: Avoiding harm in the provision of care, which includes being aware of the potential psychological and physical impacts of treatments.
- Beneficence: Acting in the best interest of the patient, which includes providing care that is culturally competent and sensitive to the unique needs of LGBTQ individuals.

Addressing Discrimination and Bias

Addressing discrimination and bias within healthcare settings is crucial for ethical practice:

- Training and education: Providing ongoing training for healthcare providers and staff to recognize and combat personal biases and institutional discrimination.
- Reporting mechanisms: Establishing clear procedures for reporting and addressing instances of discrimination or bias within the healthcare setting.

Advocacy and Policy Development

Healthcare providers can play an important role in advocating for policies that support LGBTQ health and well-being:

- Policy development: Working with professional organizations and advocacy groups to develop policies that promote LGBTQ-inclusive healthcare practices.
- Community involvement: Engaging with the LGBTQ community to understand their needs and advocate for changes that improve access to care and health outcomes.

Case Studies and Ethical Dilemmas

Exploring case studies and ethical dilemmas can provide valuable insights into the complexities of LGBTQ healthcare. Examples might include:

Case study 1: Navigating informed consent for a transgender teenager seeking hormone therapy.

Case study 2: Addressing the confidentiality concerns of a bisexual patient who has not disclosed their sexual orientation to their family.

Case study 3: Ensuring non-discriminatory access to fertility treatments for a lesbian couple.

Navigating the legal and ethical considerations in LGBTQ healthcare is essential for providing compassionate and competent care. By understanding anti-discrimination laws, ensuring informed consent and confidentiality, recognizing the importance of legal gender identity, addressing discrimination and bias, and advocating for inclusive policies, healthcare providers can better serve their LGBTQ patients.

CONCLUSION

In "Cultivating LGBTQ Sensitivity in Healthcare: A Comprehensive Guide for Providers," we have explored the myriad aspects of creating an inclusive and supportive healthcare environment for LGBTQ individuals. From understanding the historical context and health disparities faced by this community to implementing practical strategies for effective communication and ethical care, this book has provided a thorough roadmap for healthcare providers committed to enhancing the quality of care for LGBTQ patients.

As healthcare providers, advocating for and implementing these strategies is not only a professional responsibility but also a moral imperative. The insights and practical guidance provided in this book aim to equip providers with the tools necessary to deliver high-quality, inclusive care. By fostering an environment of understanding, respect, and advocacy, we can make significant strides in reducing health disparities and improving the overall well-being of LGBTQ individuals.

The journey towards LGBTQ sensitivity in healthcare is ongoing. It requires continuous learning, self-reflection, and a commitment to equity and justice. By embracing these principles, healthcare providers can contribute to a more inclusive and compassionate healthcare system where all patients, regardless of their sexual orientation or gender identity, receive the care they deserve.

REFERENCES

- Avery, A. M., Hellman, R. E., & Sudderth, L. K. (2001). *Satisfaction with care: The experience of transgender patients. Journal of Gay & Lesbian Social Services.*
- Baker, K. E., Durso, L. E., & Cray, A. (2014). *Moving the needle: The impact of the Affordable Care Act on LGBT communities. Center for American Progress.*
- Bradford, J., Reisner, S. L., Honnold, J. A., & Xavier, J. (2013). *Experiences of transgender-related discrimination and implications for health: Results from the Virginia Transgender Health Initiative Study. American Journal of Public Health.*
- Fredriksen-Goldsen, K. I., Kim, H. J., Barkan, S. E., Muraco, A., & Hoy-Ellis, C. P. (2013). *Health disparities among lesbian, gay, and bisexual older adults: Results from a population-based study. American Journal of Public Health.*
- Grant, J. M., Mottet, L. A., Tanis, J., Harrison, J., Herman, J. L., & Keisling, M. (2011). *Injustice at every turn: A report of the National Transgender Discrimination Survey. National Center for Transgender Equality and National Gay and Lesbian Task Force.*
- Institute of Medicine (IOM) (2011). *The health of lesbian, gay, bisexual, and transgender people: Building a foundation for better understanding. National Academies Press.*
- Lambda Legal (2010). *When health care isn't caring: Lambda Legal's survey on discrimination against LGBT people and people with HIV. Lambda Legal.*
- Mayer, K. H., Bradford, J. B., Makadon, H. J., Stall, R., Goldhammer, H., & Landers, S. (2008). *Sexual and gender minority health: What we know and what needs to be done. American Journal of Public Health.*

- Meyer, I. H. (2003). *Prejudice, social stress, and mental health in lesbian, gay, and bisexual populations: Conceptual issues and research evidence. Psychological Bulletin.*